THE OFFICIAL SHOP ST… D'S JOKE BOOK

Also in this series:

THE OFFICIAL IRISH JOKE BOOK
THE OFFICIAL IRISH JOKE BOOK NO. 3 (BOOK 2 TO FOLLOW)
THE OFFICIAL SCOTTISH JOKE BOOK
THE WORLD'S WORST JOKE BOOK
THE OFFICIAL AUSSIE JOKE BOOK
POSITIVELY THE LAST IRISH JOKE BOOK
THE OFFICIAL IRISH JOKE BOOK NO. 4
THE OFFICIAL ANGLER'S JOKE BOOK
DELAYED BY FOG IN TIMBUCTOO: A BOOK OF EXCUSES
THE OFFICIAL CAT LOVERS/DOG LOVERS JOKE BOOK
THE OFFICIAL SALESMAN'S JOKE BOOK
THE OFFICIAL ENGLISH, IRISH AND SCOTTISH JOKE BOOK
THE OFFICIAL GRAFFITI JOKE BOOK

Russell Lewis

The Official Shop Steward's Joke Book

Illustrated by Bill Tidy

Futura Publications Limited

A Futura Book

First published in Great Britain by
Futura Publications Limited in 1980

The cartoon *Homo-electrical-sapiens Britannicus, circa 1970* by JAK on page 7 is reproduced by kind permission of *The Evening Standard*.
The cartoon *The Old Horse Doesn't Like Being Fenced In* by LOW on page 8 is reproduced by kind permission of the LOW Trustees and Express Newspapers Limited.

ISBN 0 7088 1709 2

Filmset, printed and bound in Great Britain by
Hazell Watson & Viney Ltd
Aylesbury, Bucks

Futura Publications Limited
110 Warner Road
Camberwell, London SE5

CONTENTS

Homo-electrical-sapiens Britannicus, circa 1970.

THE OLD HORSE DOESN'T LIKE BEING FENCED IN

TUC

Too Late
'I hate negotiating,' said the union official, 'and I can't stand making speeches to the lads. As for the annual Trade Union Congress, it bores me stiff.'
'Why don't you give up?' asked the psychiatrist.
'I can't, I'm General Secretary of my union.'

Simple
Questioner: 'Now that there is fighting going on between Vietnam and Cambodia, which country should be called a threat to peace?'
Leftwing union leader: 'Chile.'

Hear, Hear
The Trade Union Congress at its annual conference unanimously passed a resolution that you must give credit to the worker with a large family – he can't live without it!

Real Poser

The TUC in its recommendations on the budget to the Chancellor of the Exchequer today said that the working men of Britain not only wanted more take-home pay but to get back more of it after it's been taken home.

Yearly Set-to

The TUC annual conference has been described as a gathering where factions speak louder than words

Auspicious Beginnings

The first Royal Commission on Trade Unions in 1861 was appointed following violence in Sheffield where union members dropped cans of gunpowder. It has been an explosive issue ever since.

Cover Blown

TUC is a powerful explosive. (Schoolboy howler)

Conversation Piece

'What do you think of the TUC as an institution?'
'OK if you like living in an institution.'

In the Family

'Is it true,' asked the daughter of the General Secretary of the TUC, 'that you spend most of your days dealing with industrial relations?'

'Yes,' said her father.

'Then how is it,' she asked, 'that you never bring any of them home?'

Keeping up with the Bloggses

A well-known TUC leader, whom we shall call Mr Bloggs, who was rather pleased with his own success in life, was once asked who he would like to be apart from himself. He thought deeply, then his eyes came to rest on his wife and he said unexpectedly, 'Mrs Bloggs's next husband.'

Advice Rarely Taken

A new miners' delegate, anxious to make a hit at conference by speaking about energy policy, consulted a veteran attender who told him, 'The union rule is – if you don't strike oil in three minutes, stop boring.'

Smooth

One young delegate who spoke for the first time at the TUC annual conference asked one of the old hands how it had gone and was pleased when told, 'That was a Rolls Royce of a speech.' Proudly recounting this to another old hand he was shattered when this one said, 'That's what he says to all the first timers. It means you were well oiled, almost inaudible and went on for a very long time.'

Success for the Surgeon

One veteran delegate to conference had an operation to cure his drinking problem – it was to take away a brass rail that had been pressing against his foot for years.

Go to Sleep

A delegate was boring the pants off everybody. He said, 'I want housing reform, I want tax reform, I want . . .' – a voice from the back of the hall, 'Chloroform!'

PRIVATE
CHLOROFORM
NHS
CHLOROFOR

Blackpool Belonged to Him

A delegate who had had too much the night before, woke up in hospital covered in bandages, with his best friend, another delegate, sitting next to the bed. 'What happened?' he asked. 'We were in the bar and you walked over to the window, got on the sill and said you were going to fly round town.' 'But why didn't you stop me? I thought you were my friend,' said the patient. 'Last night,' said his friend, 'I thought you could do it.'

Edification

Point made in the education debate: 'It's knowledge we need. Ask the average man when Magna Carta was King of England and he can't tell you.'

Question of Recognition

Overheard at Brighton conference:
'A crab bit my toe on the beach today.'
'Which one?'
'Don't know: all crabs look alike to me.'

They're All at It

'Waiter, what's this fly doing in my soup?'
'I think, sir, that he's trying to catch the Chairman's eye.'

Another Variation
During lunch at conference:
'Waiter, there's a dead fly in my soup.'
'It's all right, sir, he's not dead, he's just on strike.'

UNION BUSINESS

TUC Psalm
The Union is my shepherd; I shall not work,
It makes me to lie down on the job: it leadeth me beside the still factories.
It restoreth my fringe benefits.
It leadeth me in the paths of disruption for its own sake.
Yea though I walk through the valley of the shadow of dismissal,
I will fear no victimization: for the union is with me.
Its restrictive practices and go slows they comfort me.
It prepareth a strike committee before me in the presence of my employers.
It anointeth my head with pay rises; my bank balance runneth over.
Surely shop stewards and union dues shall follow me all the days of my membership; and I shall dwell in a council house for ever.

Last Sacrifice
'Brothers,' said the union leader seeking re-election, 'I have served you at terrific cost to my personal life, have neglected my health, my house, my wife, my children.' 'Stop,' said a member, 'you've done enough, I'm voting for the other chap.'

Might Breed Keenness
'Experiments in genetic engineering could be dangerous and could be the cause of much concern.' (Clive Jenkins, October 1978)

Closed Chapel
Union baron at wedding: 'Why do you rope off the aisles?'
Vicar: 'So that the groom can't get away.'

Wedded to the Rules
A union leader looking for his wife went to a marriage bureau. 'Is this a union shop?' he asked. 'Oh yes, where nothing's left on the shelf.'
Shown photographs of eligible females, he chose a beautiful blonde.
'I'm afraid,' said the lady, 'you'll have to have this one' – a frightful old battleaxe. 'We're working to rule and this one has seniority.'

Unpalatable Truth
'What made you lose your job with the union?'
'Stomach trouble – the members got sick of me.'

Union official: 'I hope I can count on you in the union election.'
Worker: 'No, I've promised support to another.'
Union official (knowingly): 'But promising and doing are two different things.'
Worker: 'Then I'll be happy to give you my promise.'

Hidden Influence
A member at the annual conference of the Labourers Union pointed an accusing finger at the General Secretary and said, 'I dare you to reveal the sinister interest that controls you.' 'You leave my wife out of this,' said the union chief.

What a Stiff
A delegation of enthusiastic British union officials was being shown round Moscow at the height of the 1930 purges. 'Do you have habeas corpus in the Soviet Union?' one asked. 'No,' said a British foreign correspondent who happened to accompany the party, 'but they do have habeas cadaver.'

Marked Man
Jack Williams was elected and accepted the office of shop steward. We could not get a better man. (Report in union journal)

On Union Mass Meetings
'Attendance is not representative . . . the opportunities for intimidation are limitless and no one can count the hands.' (Lord George-Brown)

SHOP STEWARDS

Shop steward: 'What are you doing?'
Assembly-line worker: 'Sharpening a pencil.'
Shop steward: 'Not allowed; that's a job for a carpenter.'

Old Fable
When shop stewards tell their children fairy stories, they begin, 'Once upon a time and a half.'

PARTICIPATION

Suggestions Welcome
As an experiment on Saturday next, the mill will be 'at home' to the public, members of which will have an opportunity to tell operatives what they can do with their machines. (Lancashire paper)

Out of the Frying Pan?
Democracy substitutes election by the incompetent many for appointment by the corrupt few. (George Bernard Shaw)

Theoretical
A worker's rights are those which belong to him which he can't have.

Demonology
Democracy is government by demons. (Schoolboy howler)

Opportunity Knocks
Democracy means simply the bludgeoning of the people by the people for the people. (Oscar Wilde)

A Russian citizen went to vote, was given a sealed envelope and shown the ballot box into which to put it.
'May I open it and see whom I'm voting for?'
'I should think not,' came the indignant reply. 'Don't you realize that this is a secret ballot?'

UNION BIGWIGS' WIT AND WISDOM

David Basnett, NUGMW
'TUC chiefs will fight any new pay curbs a Tory government imposes on them' – the Tories had already decided to abandon pay restraint. (May 1979)

'Only a high-powered team of experts can uncover the real facts about unemployment.' (November 1978)

Frank Chapple, General Secretary, ETU
'Where do you find volunteers to have their wages cut?'

Terry Duffy
'Communism strangles personal freedom and is death to democracy.'

Asked the reason for his success he said, 'I came out of the jungle.' (From shop steward to President of the AEUW in nine years)

Duffy categorized the Left whom he defeated for the leadership of the AEUW as 'Communists, Marxists, Trotskyists and Tribunites'.

'Trade unionism to me is about protecting the interests of minorities against the influence of big brother.'

Pubs, shops and restaurants open round the clock . . . and a year's paid holiday every ten years for the workers – such was the vision proclaimed by Terry Duffy when he became President Elect of the Engineering Union.

Skyscraper flats are 'the most retrograde slip ever made,' he said. 'People trapped on top of each other in those pigeon boxes are housed like animals so they behave like animals.'

Alan Fisher, NUPE
On Grunwick, 'There is more violence than I had hoped for . . . We want a peaceful picket.'

Clive Jenkins
. . . has been described as a man who goes into a revolving door behind you and comes out first.

Asked advice on what to do about the Queen's pay claim, Clive said, 'If I were the Queen's shop steward, then as a republican, I would advise a redundancy deal as well.'

One of the most potent influences on Clive Jenkins's early life was the film *Citizen Kane*. He said, 'For the first time I understood organization, powers and lust . . . I was already a trade union delegate.'

Jack Jones
According to Mike Yarwood, when Jim Callaghan asked Jack Jones if he had ever wanted to be Prime Minister, Jack replied, 'No, never, because if I ever became Prime Minister I'd have to take orders from someone like me.'

In East Germany he was reported to have said that that was where he really felt at home. Many who knew him back in Britain said what a pity it was that he didn't stay on.

Len Murray
Len Murray's constant theme since he became TUC General Secretary is that governments must consult him. He obviously doesn't know the definition of consult – to seek another's approval of a course already decided on.

Sid Weighell, General Secretary, NUR
On the situation if the Tories won the May 1979 General Election: 'I will say to the lads, come on – get your snouts in the trough.'

Arthur Scargill
Joe Gormley arrived in heaven and Peter asked him where he'd like to be quartered. 'Anywhere that I don't bump into Arthur Scargill,' he said. So Peter put him on an adjacent cloud assuring him that Arthur would not come that way. In no time he was aroused by Scargill charging by in his Volvo. Joe went to complain. 'I know what you're going to say,' said Peter, 'but that wasn't who you thought it was: it was the Boss pretending to be Arthur Scargill.'

*

DOWN TOOLS

RATE FOR THE JOB

Distributive Justice
The mother of Alan Jay Lerner, author of *Camelot* and other notable musical hits, was talking to neighbours. One said, 'Isn't your son lucky!'
'Yes,' said Mrs Lerner, 'and the odd thing is, the harder he works, the luckier he gets.'

New Rule Book
Six days shalt thou labour and on the seventh thou shalt labour longer for thou shalt be paid double time.

Forgetful
Wife: 'Did you ask for a rise today?'
Husband: 'No, it slipped my mind in the heat of the moment and amidst all the excitement about the firm going bust.'

Shortfall
'Here's your money for seven hours' loafing.'
'That's not right, it was eight and a half hours.'

All Work and No Pay

Boss: 'This machine can do the work of twenty men for a quarter of their wages: it behaves almost as if it has brains.'

Shop steward: 'Not in my book it doesn't.'

Net Result

'What's your gross income?'

'I have no gross income, only net income. I'm a fisherman.'

Pre-Beveridge

If any would not work, neither should he eat. (St Paul's Epistle to the Thessalonians)

Cheap at the Price

Lawyer: 'Do you mean to say that you charge 200 guineas for only two days' work?'

Whistler: 'No, I charge for the experience of a lifetime.'

Yawning Deficit

If time is money then everybody lives beyond his means.

Hemmed In

First printer: 'Why are you looking so miserable, didn't we have a big rise last month?'

Second printer: 'That's just it: since the last rise I earn so much I can't afford to take a day off.'

Final Reckoning

A clerk was handed, by mistake, a pay envelope which contained a blank cheque. 'Just as I feared,' he said, 'my deductions have finally overtaken my salary.'

Head Hunted

The young clerk made an appointment with his boss and immediately demanded a big rise.

Boss: 'Why should I give you it?'

Clerk: 'Because three other companies are after me.'

Boss: 'Which other companies?'

Clerk: 'The Gas Board, the Electricity Board and Post Office Telephones.'

Boss: 'Rise granted.'

Something for Everybody

Collective bargaining is, nowadays, a form of division of labour whereby management bargains and labour collects.

Not Such a Bargain
What the trades union officials mean by bargaining is that they should, in the public sector, be able to extract payment from the taxpayer, in return for services which he or she does not want. (Jo Grimond, *The Common Welfare*)

STRIKING

Moderates' Bare Majority
A strike of nude chorus girls at Raymond's Revue Bar was brought to an end after a show of hands, knees and bumpsidaisy.

Old China Hand
An electricity strike blacked out a Chinese opera. Unconcerned, the leading actor asked the audience to raise their hands in the air: the lights came on. 'You see,' he said. 'Confucius say truth – many hands make light work.'

How Times Change
Labour MP: 'What are you striking for?'
Shop steward: 'Shorter hours.'
Labour MP: 'Quite right, sixty minutes is far too long.'

ALL THOSE AGAINST?

Shock for the Bookies
In the last power station strike, electricity cuts were so severe that in the main race at Wembley Greyhound Stadium the electric hare came third.

Iron Rations
At a steelworks in Port Talbot, an industrial dispute has broken out in protest over the food served in the canteen. Apparently, it is so bad that the men want shorter dinner breaks.

1926: Second Opinion
F. E. Smith said that, when he met the coalminers' leaders, he thought they were the stupidest people he had ever met – until he met the coal owners.

What's in a Name?
When England had the world's best footballers and best workmen, the key player who scored most of the goals was called the centre forward. Now they call him the striker.

Striking Thought
If strikers often find the whole thing a quiet laugh, that is because they understand the most basic joke of all – that everything is funny which happens to somebody else.

Not Neutral
During the General Strike of 1926 the newspapers were closed by a printers' strike, so Winston Churchill decided there must be a government newspaper, the *British Gazette*, which conveyed his characteristically pugnacious message. Criticized afterwards for its lack of impartiality, he said, 'I decline utterly to be impartial as between the fire brigade and the fire.'

STRIKING SAYINGS

Nuts to NUPE
Charles Donnet, leader of the General and Municipal Workers (GMWU) said of the NUPE leader, Alan Fisher, who had been responsible for the numerous disruptions by local government workers in the winter of 1979, that he was 'a wide boy who had been run over by his own barrow'.

Glimpse of the Obvious
Ray Buckton, General Secretary of ASLEF: 'The first thing for British Rail to do is to buy some goodwill among the men, and that price is 10 per cent of about £7.'

York Ham
Sir Paul Bryan, Tory MP for Howden: 'Does the Prime Minister appreciate that in the West Riding of Yorkshire we have the biggest concentration of pigs in the country?'

Dialogue of the Deaf
Bill Dunn, shop steward of the London ambulancemen: 'This time we're determined the capital will take notice of what we're saying, and if that means lives lost, that is how it must be. We're fed up with being Cinderellas. This time we're going to the ball.'
David Ennals, Health Minister at the time: 'I do not believe that the men when they consider these issues properly and fairly will leave London without an emergency service. I cannot believe it.'

Car Window Sticker
Don't vote Labour. Vote TGWU and cut out the middleman.

Shop window in '79 Winter Crisis
Panic Buyers Welcome.

Why Not Wrap Up?
Ministry instructions to headmasters during the school caretakers' strike: 'We cannot allow you to provide packed meals as this would be regarded as a form of strike-breaking.'

Service with a Scowl
Trevor Huff, NUPE Regional Officer: 'Do precisely what is in your contract without a smile or a sparkle. It is up to the individual whether or not to smile, but I would point out that there is very little to smile about when you're earning only £42 a week.'

Appease Please
Dennis Skinner, Labour MP for Bolsover: 'The lorry strike would end immediately if the haulage bosses were told to pay the money.'

Silence is Golden
Speaker of the House of Commons: 'Order! Perhaps the House is not aware that all this noise is being broadcast.'

Really Healey
Chancellor Denis Healey: 'Recent industrial troubles are a hiccup in the Labour Government's record of successful co-operation with the trade unions.'

Patriotism is *Enough*
'I don't think that other people in the world would share the view that there is industrial chaos in Britain: Please don't run down your country.'

Information Please
Moss Evans, General Secretary of the TGWU: 'Crisis, what crisis? A ridiculous amount of hysteria has been built up in the press on this terminology called secondary picketing.'

Simplicity Itself
'I would not hesitate to cross the picket line if I believed it might do good.' (PM James Callaghan)
'I'd like to see what happened if he tried to cross this line. What James Callaghan says doesn't mean anything any more. I think next week everything will come to a stop.' (Picketing lorry driver at Tilbury Docks)

Short if Not Sweet
Tom Miles, ASLEF executive member on his members' message to London Transport: 'Get stuffed!'

Reverse Treatment
'According to our records you are a telephonist and a trade unionist. I'm sorry I'm not treating trade unionists today.' (Patrick Chesterman, orthopaedic surgeon)

Oh Well, That's All Right Then
'The only effect we are having on cancer patients and their treatment is perhaps to slow it down.' (Stephen Eaton, NUPE shop steward)

No Hurry
'As it is now a fortnight since the PM returned from the Caribbean, no one could accuse him of taking precipitate action.' (Margaret Thatcher)

Biter Bit
'If members cannot get into work tomorrow because of the weather, we may have to postpone the walkout.' (Leader of the walkout in the Navy Department at Bath)

Keeping Your Cool – Till You're Dead
'We are all threatened with malnutrition in the long run.' (James Callaghan when strikes were threatening food supplies)

SHOP CLOSING AND PICKETING

Leonardo Blocked
Home owner: '£200 for painting a room? Ridiculous, I wouldn't pay that to Leonardo da Vinci.'
Painter: 'If this bloke Leonardo does it for less, I'll picket your place.'

LEONARDO DA VINCI IS A SCAB!
MICHELANGELO
PAINTER &
DECORATOR

He Done It

Despite a large picket line outside the theatre showing an Agatha Christie whodunit, the public kept rolling up. The strike committee had a meeting and hit on a bright idea. Next day, there was only one picket next to a placard which said, 'The heroine's uncle did it.'

Irrefutable

The store in dispute with its staff during sale time had a notice up saying: BUY NOW AND SAVE 20 PER CENT. To which the pickets responded with notices saying: DON'T BUY NOW AND SAVE 100 PER CENT.

Conscience Clause

'It is indeed odd and significant that the only excuses accepted by bureaucrats for slipping out of their embrace are religious. Why, both in the context of the closed shop in industry and education . . . why cannot I have a conscience unless I belong to a religious sect?' (Jo Grimond, *The Common Welfare*)

Non-Marxist
Groucho Marx would never have approved of the closed shop. As he said, he wouldn't want to join a club that would have him as a member.

LIBBERS AND CHAUVINISTS

Drop Five
'Always remember that the people who sat around the guillotine knitting were women.' (Laurence Harvey)

Division of Labour
'For men must work and women must weep.' (Charles Kingsley, *The Three Fishers*)

Women's Lip
First wife: 'My husband's an efficiency expert.'
Second wife: 'What's that?'
First wife: 'It's like this: if women did it they'd call it nagging.'

Tip Off
Advice to employers – Never underestimate a woman unless you're discussing her age or her weight.

Definition
Career woman – One who would rather go out and take orders than stay at home and be boss.

Women at Work
A hoarding bore an advertisement from a firm of accountants: 'Course in Accounting for Women.' But some wit had scrawled underneath: 'There is no accounting for women.'

Sex Deficiency
The woman's work that's never done is usually the bit she asked her man to do.

Voice from the Past
A woman's preaching is like a dog walking on his hind legs; it is not done well, but you are surprised to find it done at all. (Dr Samuel Johnson)

Men and Amonnensis
An optimist is a man who marries his secretary under the impression he can go on dictating to her.

Taking it Sitting Down
A man tried to offer his seat on the bus to a lady who three times thrust him back into his seat assuring him she was a working woman, a women's libber and had no time for this false gallantry. The fourth time, he said, 'You really must let me get up this time – I'm two miles away from my stop already.'

Preferably Scented
Working single lady wants digs, must have bath; urgently. (Advert in *Sheffield Star*)

So That's Why
The reason why women are said to drive more slowly than men is that they will do anything to stay under thirty.

Since Revised
Nature has given women so much power that the law has very wisely given them little. (Dr Johnson)

Just Natural Courtesy
'Dear me,' said the managing editor's wife at the end of a waltz with one of the staff at the firm's annual hop, 'I'm danced out.'
'Oh, I wouldn't say that,' said her partner gallantly, 'just pleasantly plump.'

Faiblesse Oblige
'You can't help liking my boss,' said the worker, 'if you don't, he gives you the sack.'

Now You Come to Mention It
When a man's really keen on hard work the odds are that he's an employer.

Ruthless
Boss: 'I've had my eye on you: you're capable, thorough and ambitious.'
Executive: 'Thank you.'
Boss: 'That is why I'm going to give you the sack. It's men like you who start up rival companies.'

Quids In

Boss: 'There's ten pounds gone from my drawer, Jimmy. The only people with keys to that drawer are you and I.'

Jimmy: 'What d'you say we each chip in a fiver and say no more about it?'

Labour

A time and motion expert went to his boss about his holiday and came out furious. He said, 'The boss's view is that I am so efficient that I could enjoy myself as much in one week as the average person can in two, so a week is all I get.'

Wheels Within Wheels

First bloated capitalist: 'I've solved my lateness problem by giving all my workers a car.'

Second bloated capitalist: 'How does that make any difference?'

First bloated capitalist: 'They have to get there early to find a parking space.'

Three in One

A worker asked his boss for a raise. 'After all, I'm doing three men's work,' he said. 'Do tell me who the other two are,' said his employer, 'and I'll sack them.'

Double Indemnity

Boss: 'Jones, after the office party yesterday you were seen wheeling a dog cart down Piccadilly. Don't you think that can knock our company's prestige?'

Assistant: 'It never occurred to me. After all, you were in the dog cart.'

Limbering Up

Boss: 'You've idled away the whole afternoon, why are you so keen to get home early?'

Aide: 'I want to start working on the lawn.'

The Right Spirit

Boss of public relations firm in speech to executives: 'Finally, don't go drinking vodka with clients because vodka doesn't stay on your breath. Drink gin instead: I'd rather they thought you were drunk than stupid.'

Conspiracy of Silence

Boss: 'Your salary is a personal matter not to be divulged to anyone.'

New executive: 'I shan't say a word: I'm just as ashamed of it as you are.'

All Right for Some

Tax inspector: 'What's this claim for a trip to Nice for medical reasons?'
Managing director: 'That's because my creditors wouldn't let me breathe here.'

Catch 22

Employer: 'If you work for us you'll have Christmas bonus, share bonus, private health insurance, night school and day release courses, use of company car and a subsidized mortgage.'
Applicant: 'Fine, but what d'you pay?'
Employer: 'Surely you don't expect wages as well!'

Cheap at the Price

'I'm sorry you'll have to leave us,' said the boss, 'but it may cheer you to learn that it's costing us £200,000 to get a computer in your place.'

Labour Intensive

The rich industrialist asked his young son what he wanted for Christmas. 'A baby brother,' was the reply.
'But it's only a fortnight to Christmas: there's not enough time.'
'Can't you put more men on the job?'

Peter Principle
'The trouble with senior management is that there are too many one ulcer men doing two ulcer jobs.' (Prince Philip, May 1963)

Anxious
An economics graduate was offered the chance of a lifetime as personal assistant to a financier. Eagerly he asked the terms.
Financier: 'You receive £10,000 a year for making every worry of mine your own.'
Graduate: 'Fine, but where's the £10,000 coming from?'
Financier: 'That's your first worry.'

One of the High Ups
'They tell me the boss's son started at the bottom of the ladder.'
'Yes, but when he took his first step, the ladder had been placed on the top storey.'

Economics of Undertaking
Enquirer: 'Is business lively?'
Undertaker: 'No, the people are lively, and my business is dying.'

Embarrassed
Boss: 'Why do you want a raise?'
Worker: 'Sir, I wouldn't ask but my kids have been at me ever since they found that other families eat three times a day.'

Alluring Prospect
By working faithfully eight hours a day, you may eventually get to be a boss and work twelve hours a day. (Robert Frost)

Scruples
A friend of Henry Ford was asked whether the great car-maker was a religious man. 'Oh yes,' said the friend, 'he watches over the spiritual well-being of his workers, and if any one of them so much as misbehaves with a woman, he immediately gets the sack.'

None so Blind
Secretary: 'The invisible man is here.'
Boss: 'I can't see him.'

Always Bridge that Gap
In any office you can always tell the executive. He's the chap who can take a two-hour lunch on any day of the week without being missed.

IDLE HANDS

Standing up for Their Rights
'I don't understand why they erected statues on that building.'
'They're not statues: they're bricklayers.'

Dead Right
A rat catcher was sacked by the Town Clerk. Asked why, he said, 'Nothing personal: you just lack the killer instinct.'

Somnolent
Boss: 'You're late again; why?'
Clerk: 'Sorry, I overslept.'
Boss: 'What, d'you sleep at home too?'

" I'D GET A CAT BUT IT WANTS TIME AND A HALF! "

Mystery Solved

'Why don't you answer the telephone?' asked the manager of his secretary in an exasperated tone.

'I just get fed up,' she said. 'Nine times out of ten it's for you.'

Time and Motion

Many workers in British industry are already on a four-day week. They just take five days to get through it!

Full Circle

The social worker seeing a tramp lying in the sun asked: 'Why don't you get a job?'

'Why?'

'To have some money in the bank.'

'Why?'

'So that when you had enough you could retire and stop working.'

'I'm not working now.'

Job Satisfaction

'I like work; it fascinates me. I can sit and look at it for hours.' (Jerome K. Jerome)

Abstinence

Foreman: 'Don't you ever feel like work?'
Lazy worker: 'Yes, but I do without.'

No Time Off for Pain

'What's hurting?'
'There's a splinter in my foot.'
'Why don't you pull it out?'
'What, in my own time? Not bloody likely!'

To Work is to Prey

'Are you seeking work, my man?'
'No, but I'd like a well-paid job.'

Cut-off Point

Employer: 'Where have you been?'
Labourer: 'Having a haircut.'
Employer: 'You can't have your haircut in my time.'
Labourer: 'Why not? It grew in your time!'

Timely Observation

Employer: 'Are you a clock watcher?'
Applicant: 'No, I'm one for the open air myself, I'm a hooter-listener.

Quick Extract
The fitter was a patient man but his mate was so lazy that after a couple of months he could contain himself no longer. 'Bill,' he said, 'I'm sick and tired of seeing you there with both hands in your pockets. For God's sake take one of them out.'

Pro Bono Publico
Notice to all employees: Some time between starting and quitting time, without infringing on lunch periods, coffee breaks, rest periods, story-telling, ticket-selling, holiday planning and the re-capping of yesterday's TV programmes, we ask that each employee try to find some time for a work break. This may seem radical, but it may aid steady employment, assure regular pay cheques. (Specimen Chevrolet Co. of New York)

Full Employment
It takes two men to unload a piece of machinery at the works in central Scotland but at Grangemouth docks the same task needs twenty dockers.

Unique
Perhaps man is the only being who can properly be called idle. (Dr Samuel Johnson)

Simple Cure
'When I feel like exercising, I just lie down till the feeling goes away.' (Paul Terry)

This is the Buzz
A bee is never as busy as it sounds – it just doesn't know how to buzz any slower.

Curious
Boss: 'You should have been here at 8.30.'
Worker: 'Why, did anything unusual happen?'

Overhaul Needed
Gasman calling at a house: 'I hear you have an old geyser here that's not working?'
Wife: 'Yes, he's down at the Ministry of Employment office collecting his dole.'

Lazy Latin
After examination the man said, 'Look here, Doc, just tell me in plain language what's wrong and none of your fancy Latin names.'
'All right,' said the doctor. 'You're just lazy.'
'In that case,' said the man, 'let's have the long Latin name so that I can tell my wife.'

IMMIGRANTS

Flying Start

'I'm a coloured one-eyed Jew – do I need anything else?' (Sammy Davis Jnr)

First Things First

Teacher: 'What are the main races in Britain?'
Bookie's son: 'The Derby, the Oaks and the Grand National.'

Proven Liar

Pat was up on a charge of being drunk.
'Who gave you the whiskey, Pat?'
'If you please, your honour, it was a Scotsman who gave me a whole bottle.'
'Two hundred pounds for perjury,' said the judge.

*

ON THE JOB

IN THE WORKS

Deus ex Machina
Bishop: 'What are you trying to do?'
Worker priest: 'I'm taking God into industry.'
Bishop: 'How interesting for Him, where d'you plan to take Him next?'

Antidote
A very pretty girl who worked in the trainees' canteen was perpetually asked for her phone number. She solved the problem by giving the number of a pest control agency – the chaps usually got the point.

Industrial Relations
In some firms everyone gets on like the members of a big family: in others they get on quite well.

Advice to New Recruits
You are completely dispensable – except when you want a day off.

Goodwill All Round
Industry is full of willing people – those who are willing to work and those who are willing to let them.

Safety at Work
Inspector: This machine should have a warning on it not to go too near.'
Manager: 'Yes, we used to have one but no one ever got hurt so we took it down.

Golden Boy
Manager: 'Can't understand why the men don't like me. When I left my last place they gave me a solid silver tray.'
Foreman: 'Don't worry; if you'd only leave here I can guarantee you a gold one.'

Legal Drop-out
Workman – as solicitor hands him a cheque for £30 out of £100 received for damages – 'I'm wondering who fell off the scaffolding, you or me?'

Non-metric
Housewife: 'A ton of coal, please.'
Coalman: 'What size?'
Housewife: 'If it's all the same with you a ton weighing 2240 pounds.'

Faulty Premise
Foreman: 'You know you shouldn't smoke when you're working.'
Assembly-line worker: 'Who says I'm working?'

Misplaced
Plumber: 'Good morning, madam, here I am ready to fix the hot water system and I haven't left a single tool behind.'
Housewife: 'There's nothing wrong with my hot water. You must have come to the wrong address.'

Backward Step
'You look a bit the worse for wear, what's happened?'
'I just bet Bill he couldn't carry me on his back to the top of the ladder – and I won.'

Shoulders to the Wheel

A worker was caught in a big wheel and whirled round seven times before being flung off. The foreman rushed up distressed and said, 'Speak to me, speak to me.'

'Why should I?' asked the worker. 'I've just passed you seven times running and you didn't say a word.'

BANKING

Germinal Thought

The clerks were cashing their salary cheques. 'I hope you don't mind the microbes,' said the cashier as he handed out rather soiled notes. 'Don't worry,' said the recipient, 'on my salary not even a microbe could survive.'

Last Lap

The Bank Director asked a new clerk why the cashier had gone to the races during the hours of business. 'He told me it was his last chance to get the books to balance,' said the clerk.

Don't Bank on It

A bank cashier was approached by his nineteen-year-old daughter who said darkly, 'Don't you think you'd better get another job; I think your bank's in trouble.'

'Whatever makes you think that?' he asked.

'Oh,' she said, 'I got a £10 cheque returned by it the other day marked "No Funds".'

Credit Where It's Due

A bank personnel officer in Brazil wrote to his opposite number in a London bank for a reference on a job applicant called James Smith. He wrote, 'I understand that Mr Smith was a tried and trusted employee of yours.' Back came the reply, 'Mr Smith, I'm sorry to say, was trusted and he will be tried if he ever has the temerity to return to Britain.'

Quid Pro Coal

A confidence trickster tried to borrow £50 from a coalminer who politely but firmly refused, saying, 'It's due to an arrangement I have with the bank.'

'What's that?' asked the con man.

'Well,' said the miner, 'we've got an agreement that if I don't lend money the bank won't dig coal.'

At closing time in the bank twenty £1,000 notes were missing. The tellers worked all night to find them but in vain. One girl reported for work and learnt what happened. 'Oh, it's all right,' she said, 'I took them home to show my family the kind of work I'm doing.'

Banker: 'How dare you tell me you had eight years' experience as a teller when you hadn't had any?'
Recruit: 'I thought a teller was a man who told tall tales.'

Speak No Evil
'How much money did my husband draw out last week?'
'I can't divulge that. I'm sorry.'
'You're the teller aren't you?'
'Yes, but that's one thing I'm not allowed to tell.'

BROKING

Golden Rule
'If you want to be happy,' said the stockbroker to the new recruit, 'learn to live within your means – even if you have to borrow money to do so.'

Half Marx
Stockbrokers of the world unite! You have nothing to lose but your bonds.

Memo to a Whitehall Mandarin
Man is seldom so harmlessly occupied as when he is making money. (Dr Johnson)

CLERKING

How Tactful
'I really don't know how I'm going to manage without you,' said the boss to his assistant, 'but starting on the first of next month I'm going to try.'

Ambition Thwarted
Wife: 'Did you ask about promotion?'
Husband: 'No, sorry, I forgot; probably due to all the excitement when I got the sack.'

A clerk in the sales department who was asked to say grace said: 'Dear Lord, we are in receipt of your valued custom of recent date. We hope to give you satisfaction and to retain the courtesy of your continued custom in anticipation of your favourable report, we remain, your obedient servant. Amen.'

'It's time I gave up my job as a filing clerk,' said the girl at lunch.
'Why d'you say that?' asked her companion.
'Because with this alphabet soup I just find myself starting with A and going on in order all the way through to Z.'

FARMING

Night Shift
The new farm worker was wakened at 4 a.m. by the farmer who announced that they were going to cut oats. The farm worker asked, 'Are they wild oats?'
'No, of course not,' said the farmer. 'Why do you ask?'
'Because,' said the farm worker, 'if they're not wild, why do we have to go sneaking up on them in the dark?'

Getting Shot of Her
A hill farm worker from Wales went to a solicitor to get his marriage annulled. Asked on what grounds he said that her father didn't have a licence for the shotgun.

" IGNORE THE BITES. HE HAD A LICENSE FOR THE SHEEPDOG!"

No Input
A farmer brought home a horse he had bought at the market but it refused to eat or drink. 'My gosh,' said the farmer, 'if he's a good worker, I've got a bargain.'

HAIRDRESSING

Search for Fee
The baldheaded customer complained that he was being charged the same as a man with a full head of hair. The barber said, 'You don't understand. In your case we charge not for cutting the hair but for finding it before cutting.'

HOTELLING

Inniquitous
Daughter: 'Father, have you heard? They've caught the biggest hotel thief in London.'
Father: 'Which hotel was he managing?'

Lady: 'Can you give me a room and bath?'
Clerk: 'I can give you a room, madam, but you'll have to bath yourself.'

It Tolls for Thee
Page boy: 'Did you ring, sir?'
Angry guest: 'No, I was tolling. I thought you were dead.'

MINING

Black non-market
One fifth of all coal supplied for domestic purposes goes as perks to the employees of the Coal Board.

NURSING

Perceptive
First nurse: 'Why does the X-ray specialist keep dating Nurse Williams? She's so plain.'
Second nurse: 'I suppose he sees something in her that others can't.'

Hospital Poster
PLEASE HELP OUR NURSES HOME

Ultimate Cure
Matron: 'If you found a man bleeding badly from a wound in the head, what would you do?'
Trainee nurse: 'Apply a tourniquet to his neck.'

Barely Believable
A gorgeous girl lay in a hospital bed covered only in a sheet. A brisk young man came in, took off the sheet and examined her closely. 'Will you need to operate?' she asked. 'You'll have to ask the doctor that,' he said, 'I'm only the window cleaner.'

Out-Patient
'Doctor, my trouble is that people keep ignoring me.'
'Next please.'

Never a Dull Moment
Vacancies exist for two female physiotherapists, preferably with some experience. Varied work embracing in-patients and out-patients in units in Dundee and Angus. (Ad in medical journal)

A Turn for the Nurse
Anxious wife: 'Tell me honestly, is my husband making any progress?'
Pretty nurse: 'No, and he never will – he's not my type.'

Very Matey
Many Americans still think that socialized medicine means women getting together to talk about their operations.

Doctor: 'Nurse, where's the patient gone who was in this bed?'
Nurse: 'It's all right; he couldn't get warm so I put him in bed with the lady who's running a temperature of 104°.'

Pregnant Pause
A woman got into a cab and asked the driver: 'Please take me to St Mary's Hospital Maternity Ward – but don't hurry, I just work there.'

PLUMBING

Go Slow
Plumber: 'Sorry I'm late; hope you got on all right.'
Housewife: 'Oh yes, fine; while I was waiting I taught the children to swim.'

Top of the Form
Plumber: 'Where are your references?'
Applicant: 'I left them at home.'
Plumber: 'You'll do.'

Plumb Crazy
Plumber: 'Have you brought all your tools?'
New boy: 'Yes, all of them.'
Plumber: 'You fool.'

REPORTING

Fellow Professionals
Reporter interviewing a prisoner in his cell: 'If you don't mind, I'll just take a few notes?'
Prisoner: 'Careful, that's all I did and they put me in here.'

Just Average
Only a mediocre writer is always at his best. (W. Somerset Maugham)

Ghostly Error
A trade union leader hired a ghost writer to produce articles for newspapers which appeared under the trade union leader's name and had considerable success. The ghost fell ill and a substitute was found. Glancing through a draft article the union leader looked dismayed and said: 'This is not up to my usual standard.'

Both Right
'I'll bet each of these conflicting allegations about me comes from an "unimpeachable source".' (Robert Menzies speaking to the Journalists' Club in Sydney, Australia)

No Paperweight
An editor is a man with a small desk and a big wastepaper basket.

None Knew Better

Journalism – a profession whose business it is to explain to others what it personally does not understand. (Lord Northcliffe)

Now We Know

Journalism consists largely in saying 'Lord Jones; dead' to people who never knew that Lord Jones was alive. (G. K. Chesterton)

Editor: 'This isn't clear. You must learn to write so that the stupidest person can understand.'
Reporter: 'Right, sir. Now what exactly is it that you don't understand?'

Cannibal chief: 'What were you before my men captured you?'
Prisoner: 'A journalist.'
Cannibal chief: 'An editor?'
Prisoner: 'No, just a sub-editor.'
Cannibal chief: 'Cheer up, after supper you may well be editor in chief.'

Some Hope
A leader writer is an optimist who thinks he can make you think. (John A. Lincoln)

Now it's the TUC
The gallery which the reporters sit in in Parliament has become the fourth estate of the realm. (T. B. Macaulay)

Superfluous
You cannot hope to bribe or twist
(Thank God) the British journalist
But seeing what the man will do
Unbribed, there's no occasion to. (Humbert Wolfe)

Open Mind
Possible! Is anything impossible? Read the newspapers! (Duke of Wellington)

Front Man
Editor: 'You want to be a proofreader, eh. You know what that entails?'
Applicant: 'Yes, whenever you make any mistakes in the paper I take the blame.'

Meat and Right
'Hey, butcher, I'll tell you how to sell more meat.'
'How?'
'By not giving short weight.'

Opportunist
Female voice on phone: 'Do you sell maternity dresses?'
Estate agent whom she has rung in error: 'No, but can I interest you in a larger house?'

If You Want to Get Ahead
A salesman always wore his hat when he was working at his desk. When asked why, he said it was to remind himself that he had no business there.

Add My Cut
Small child: 'What does two times two make?'
Lew Grade: 'Buying or selling?'

Failure
He couldn't sell a glass of water in the Sahara desert.

Customers Come Last
Notice in department store: 'Go easy on the salesgirls; they're harder to come by than customers.'

Acid Test
Did you hear of the salesman who had the sack because his ulcer healed and his boss thought he'd lost interest in his work?

Outside Interests
Bill: 'What's it like being a salesman?'
Jack: 'It's great, I've had a marvellous time staying at fine hotels and meeting lots of wonderful people. The part I don't like is calling on the shopkeepers.

Dear Economy
In pursuit of more miles to the gallon the customer asked after the newest kind of mini car. Told the price, he said, 'That's as much as a normal size car.'
'True,' said the salesman, 'but if you want economy you have to pay for it.'

Working Her Way Up
Customer: 'How did you become a masseuse?'
Masseuse: 'In school I was always at the bottom of my class so I just naturally drifted into it.'

Wrong Plaice
'Waiter, I've tasted fresher fish than this.'
'Maybe, sir, but not 'ere you 'aven't.'

No Need for a Dust Up
'Just look at this dust, Maria, it must be all of three months old.'
'Nothing to do with me, madam, I've only been here for a fortnight.'

It Takes a Thief
'Our new maid is dishonest.'
'What proof have you?'
'Two of the towels I pinched from Gleneagles are missing.'

Pagan Ritual
Hostess: 'When the guests sit down please serve the food from the left and take away the dirty plates from the right.'
New maid: 'Why, are you superstitious?'

Couldn't Stomach Him
'How long was your last chef with you?'
'He was never with us. He was against us.'

Too Familiar
After twenty years' service Mary suddenly gave in her notice. Her employer was most distressed and said, 'Why, we've always treated you like one of the family?'
Says Mary, 'That's exactly why I'm leaving.'

SHOWBIZ

Flaming Revolution
During the last electricians' strike the London show *Oh! Calcutta!* was temporarily renamed *Fanny by Gaslight*.

What a Bore!

The man who was employed as a human cannonball in a circus decided to quit and told the owner. 'You can't do this to me,' said the owner. 'Where am I going to find another man of your calibre?'

No Business Like It

Two old friends met after twenty years, one rich, the other poor. The first one owned thirty stores and asked the other exactly what his job was. He said, 'I go round with a shovel and pick up the animals' droppings.' The rich man, shocked, immediately offered him a job as manager of one of his stores. 'What,' was the reply, 'and leave show business?'

Men of the Right Calibre

The tightrope walker had a drink problem and kept falling off the rope. Eventually he picked himself up and got a job as a human cannonball – that way everybody was happy for him to get loaded seven days a week.

♪ "THERE'S NO BUSINESS LIKE SHOW BUSINESS..
THUD!

Extended Sentence

The little boy was in tears. 'Why are you crying?' asked the teacher kindly.
'Because I have to stay in school till I'm sixteen.'
'Don't worry,' said the teacher, 'think of me, I have to stay here till I'm sixty-five.'

Pre-requisite

'Do you think Miss Smith could be a good teacher?'
'She'd be all right if she had a little class.'

Sin of Omission

Boy: 'Sir, can I be punished for what I haven't done?'
Master: 'Of course not.'
Boy: 'I haven't done my homework, sir.'

Short Handed

Education has been defined as the ability to describe a glamorous girl without using your hands.

Knowing
Teacher: 'How old would a person be who was born in 1920?'
Bright pupil: 'Man or woman?'

Unexciting Prospect
Teacher's report: 'This young lad is dull but steady – should make a good parent.'

No Future
Teacher: 'What tense is "I am beautiful"?'
Pupil: 'Past historic.'

Shockproof
A teacher is one who takes a lot of live wires and brings them down to earth.

Eager
Indignant teacher's letter to parents: 'Not only is he the worst behaved child in school – he has the best attendance record.'

Pyramiding
In today's schools the teacher is afraid of the headmaster; the headmaster is afraid of the Inspector; the Inspector is afraid of the Ministry; the Ministry is afraid of the Minister; the Minister is afraid of the parents; the parents are afraid of the children; and the children are afraid of no one.

Class Hatred
The dominant motive of some teachers.

Basic Lesson
An advertisement appeared in an educational journal – Because you're a teacher you can borrow £1,000. Many teachers wrote in saying, 'I'd like the loan because I'm a teacher and for the same reason I can't pay it back.'

Exemplary
'Wot I sez abaht eddication,' said the chairman of the Board of Governors, 'is it don't do the nippers no 'arm.'

Males Voice Choice
'Essex teachers have been urged to encourage more boys to sing in school choirs and not show preference for girls.' (Evening paper)

PLAYBOY

TRAINING

A True Believer
Training is everything. The peach was once a bitter almond; cauliflower is nothing but a cabbage with a college education. (Mark Twain)

Little Shaver
Ticked off for not sending his twelve-year-old son to school the father said it didn't matter whether his son was educated or not as he intended to make him a barber.

Bang On
'Has Johnny got a job yet?'
'Yes, he's started as a trainee in a fireworks factory.'
'How's he progressing?'
'So far, his reports have been first rate.'

TRANSPORTING

Mechanic (to lady driver whose car won't start): 'The trouble is your battery – it's flat.'
Lady driver: 'Oh dear, what shape should it be then?'

So-long, Henry

'Conductor,' complained the passenger on a bus, 'there's a lunatic sitting near me who thinks he's Henry VIII.'

'I'll soon get rid of him,' said the conductor and rang the bell, shouting, 'Next stop Hampton Court.'

What's Yours is Mine

When the railways were nationalized, engine drivers in Merthyr Tydfil wrote on the trucks, 'These are ours now.' Now they won't have any truck with that sort of thing.

Stuck Up

A lady poked a bus driver with her umbrella. 'Is that the Post Office?' she asked.

'No, ma'am,' said the driver, 'that's my ribs.'

Other Half Fare

In a cloudburst a society lady hopped on a London bus and said, 'I haven't been on a bus in ten years; I usually take a taxi or my own car.'

'Words can't express,' said the ticket collector, 'how much we've missed you.'

Generation Adrift
'Pass farther down the compartment, please.'
'But this isn't Father it's Grandfather.'

TYPING

Ongoing
Boss: 'Why were you three quarters of an hour late again today? Don't you know what time work starts in this office?'
Secretary: 'Come to think of it, no, everybody's always working when I get in.'

Poised for Action
A secretary is a girl you pay to learn to type while she is searching for a husband.

What a Carry-on
After three years in the Croydon office of a big insurance company a girl was transferred to the London HQ. The boss called her in on arrival and said, 'I hope you'll like it here, the work will be just the same as in Croydon.'
'Fine,' she said, 'kiss me and let's get started.'

'Really,' said the stockbroker to his secretary after looking over a financial statement she had typed and which he was sending to a client, 'do you count on your fingers?'
'My trouble is,' she said, 'that I'm at the awkward age. I'm too old to count on my fingers and too young to count on my legs.'

The Young Idea
The latest market research shows conclusively that only a minority of secretaries want to marry their boss: most of them would prefer to marry his son.

Hot on the Trail
A boss suspected his female staff were leaving early when he wasn't there. One day, he came back without warning and found it was just as he thought. Next morning he confronted one of the girls and said loud enough to be heard by everyone, 'Miss Snooks, yesterday I came back at five o'clock, felt your seat and it wasn't warm.'

Off Limits
Secretary, advising her replacement during her annual holiday: 'When I'm away, just carry on as I have – except with the boss.'

Positively Punishing

Boss No 1: 'My secretary is a masochist.'
Boss No 2: 'How do you know?'
Boss No 1: 'I drove her home the other night: she asked me in for a drink and then said, "Do you mind if I go and slip into something uncomfortable?" '

Be Prepared

Boss: 'Are you doing anything on Sunday evening?'
Beautiful secretary (hopefully): 'No.'
Boss: 'Then it shouldn't be hard for you to get in on time Monday morning.'

Awkward

First secretary: 'Does your boss pace up and down the office when he is dictating letters?'
Second secretary: 'I should think not, otherwise I'd fall off his lap.'

Late Entrant

'I hear you've found the very latest thing in secretaries.'
'She's all of that: she never gets here till ten.'

" WE ACKNOWLEDGE RECEIPT OF YOUR MARK II SECRETARY LAP HOLDER... "

Punctilious
Employer: 'I must tell you that I'm very keen on punctuation.'
New secretary: 'Don't worry, I'll always get here on time.'

Resigned
'That's a very ritzy fur coat for a struggling typist like you,' said the boss.
'I've stopped struggling.'

Absence Guarantee
Boss: 'After you told my wife I wouldn't be home till late, what did she say?'
Secretary: 'She said, "Can I depend on that?" '

WAITING

Plenty of Protein
'Waiter, there's a fly in my soup.'
'You're lucky, the meat course hasn't even begun yet.'

Post No Bills
Customer: 'I can't pay the bill.'
Waiter: 'Never mind, sir, I'll write your name on the wall till you come back and pay it.'
Customer: 'But then everyone will see it.'
Waiter: 'Not with your overcoat covering it.'

Popular Pronouncement
'In my forty years in this job,' said the veteran waiter, 'I've only heard one after-dinner speech which gave total satisfaction.'
'And what was that?'
'It went like this: "Waiter, bring me the bill." '

Cover Up
Waiter: 'Could you settle the bill, sir, we're just closing.'
Customer: 'But I haven't been served yet.'
Waiter: 'In that case there'll be just the cover charge.'

Stop them Beefing
'Girls,' said the restaurant manager, 'today I want you to look extra smart and sexy.'
'Is something special on?' asked the head waitress.
'No,' said the manager, 'the beef is tough.'

*

SLUMP

Unforgivable

The unemployed man who stole two coats to keep his children from freezing to death in the cold winter was arrested and brought to court. When the circumstances were explained the judge asked the shop keeper if he wanted to press charges.
'Yes,' he said sternly.
'But this man isn't a criminal,' said the judge, 'why are you so keen to go on with the case?'
'If he'd done it last week or next week I wouldn't mind,' said the shop keeper, 'but this week I'm stocktaking.'

Despatching the Redundant

When telephone directors become obsolete they are sold to wastepaper companies for conversion into pulp. They are torn in two lengthwise, then chopped into small bits in a powerful machine. (American newspaper)

Vocation

'I am in Her Majesty's Service,' said a man facing charges in a Mansfield court. 'I am on the dole.'

Fishy Story
During the World Economic Conference in London in 1933 called to discuss the international slump, the delegates were asked to a lavish dinner by the City livery companies at the Fishmongers Hall but few turned up. Most of them it seems were afraid they would only get fish and chips and the American delegates were apprehensive that if they went they might be manoeuvred into advertising fresh cod.

Expensive Right to Work
Finding that government job-creating support to an aluminium smelter would cost £200,000 of taxpayers' money per job, an MP suggested that industry ministers concerned in such projects should show their confidence in them by committing say ten per cent of their personal liquid assets to them. Strange to relate the suggestion was never taken up.

Final Dive
In the crash of 1929 receptionists in hotels in downtown New York were said to be asking guests whether they wanted their room for sleeping or jumping. Two men jumped hand in hand from a high window in the Ritz. They had a joint account.

JOB HUNTING

Interviewer: 'Sign here.'
Applicant: 'I can't write, can I make my cross?'
Interviewer: 'All right – but why two crosses, what does the second stand for?'
Applicant: 'Ph.D.'

Great Expectations
Job advertisement: 'Mammoth Enterprises is looking for keen, energetic executives aged between twenty-five and thirty-five with forty years' experience.

Reports from the Job Front
Advertisement: You can go places as a prune taster – about once every five minutes.

Comedown
Applicant: 'I like the job but the last place paid more, and gave overtime bonuses, holidays with pay, and sabbaticals.'
Employer: 'Why did you leave?'
Applicant: 'The firm went bust.'

Not So Automatic
Applicant: 'If I take this job, will I get a rise every year?'
Employer: 'Yes, If you do a good job.'
Applicant: 'I knew there was a snag somewhere.'

Two Finger Sign
Before applying for a job a shy young man first went to a fortune-teller. Noting that the crystal ball had two holes in it close together, he asked why. 'Because,' said the fortune-teller, 'on Sunday nights I go bowling.'

Muddling Through
The best way to keep a new job is to get things so mixed up on the first day that they can't afford to sack you.

A Near Thing
Boss: 'D'you know when you came closest to perfection?'
Assistant: 'No, when?'
Boss: 'When you filled out your job application.'

Quick Reference

During the Crimean War Lord Panmui the War Minister wrote to the Commander in Chief saying, 'I commend to your notice my nephew Dowbiggin, if there is a post available and if he is fit.' This was sent by the newly introduced telegraph and the telegraph clerks, who were allowed to abbreviate messages when necessary, transmitted this as 'Look after Dowb'.

Productivity Specialist

A man who had travelled to London for a job interview received a telegram saying his wife had borne quins. He immediately went over to the personnel manager and asked for a post with a high salary. 'What can you do, sir, keep accounts, drive, speak foreign languages?'

'None of those things.'

'Well, what can you do?'

'Read this telegram.'

Miss Blank

Personnel officer: 'How are your speeds?'

Secretary: 'For typing nothing special but I can talk eighty words a minute.'

First Things First

Three girls applied for the job of secretary to the director and a psychologist put to them one main question which was, 'How much is two and two?'

'Four,' said one. 'Forty-four,' said the second. 'Four or maybe forty-four,' said the third.

'There,' said the psychologist, 'the first showed logic, the second imagination, the third showed both. Which do you choose?'

The director said, 'We choose the blonde with the big tits.'

Warning Streak

Head of secretarial school: 'We insist above all on thoroughness and accuracy.'

Beautiful student: 'What about speed?'

Head: 'Out of last year's intake of fifty, twenty-one girls married their employers in the first six months.'

Virtue Unrewarded

Personnel officer: 'Why did your last boss sack you?'

Secretary: 'For the mistake I wouldn't make.'

Blast Off
Psychologist job adviser: 'Count up to ten.'
Client: '10, 9, 8, 7, ...'
P.J.A.: 'Stop, I recommend you find a job in the space programme.'

Employer: 'Where are your references?'
Applicant: 'I tore them up.'
Employer: 'What a silly thing to do.'
Applicant: 'You wouldn't say so if you knew what they said.'

Stiff Upper Lip
Dental mechanic twenty years standing seeks suitable position. (Small ad)

Spoke with Conviction
'Are you fit for really hard labour?'
'Some of the best judges in the country have taken that view.'

Going for Growth
City printers seek works manager, medium sized but expanding.

On Sale

Asked for a recommendation of a previous employee who had applied for a job as a salesman, the personnel manager said, 'I'm afraid we found Mr Jones a bit of a romancer: even the wool he tried to pull over our eyes was half cotton.'

Lesson of Experience

Lady at kitchen door: 'You know you'd stand a better chance of a job if you shaved, had a hair-cut and cleaned yourself up.'

Tramp: 'Yes ma'am, I found that out some years ago.'

Black Belt Preferred

Tea Room Attendant required. Knowledge of first aid essential. (Ad in *Northern Daily Mail*)

No Time To Waste

WANTED IMMEDIATELY: A woman for boiling down. Apply Blank Potted Incat Company. (Ad in New Zealand paper)

Cool Appraisal
Foreman: 'Where did you learn to fell trees?'
Applicant: 'In the Sahara.'
Foreman: 'But there aren't any trees in the Sahara.'
Applicant: 'Not now there aren't.'

Time-lag
Boss: 'Why were you discharged from your last place?'
Applicant: 'For good behaviour.'
Boss: 'How can that be?'
Applicant: 'They took two months off my sentence.'

TRENDY TRIBUNALS

In the Rough
Tribunal chairman: 'I suppose you know the nature of an oath?'
Golf club employee: 'After caddying for you so many times, I certainly do.'

A barrister, who was muttering impatiently as he heard what he considered a preposterous summing up at an Industrial Tribunal hearing before which he had appeared, was asked by the chairman: 'Are you trying to show your contempt for the court?' 'No,' said the barrister, 'I was trying to conceal it.'

OK
If there is a dispute between a musician and myself, it is settled amicably. I win. (Danny Kaye)

Each Way Loser
A businessman who had been taken to court several times by employees for unjust dismissal summed up the employers' prospects – 'To win is expensive, to lose is ruinous.'

THE LEISURE PROBLEM

Why Not a Seven-day Weekend?
A three-day weekend could be one way of solving unemployment problems created by micro chip technology, said scientific workers' leader Clive Jenkins in May 1979.

Down With Utopia
Every attempt in the history of the world to establish a loafer's paradise has wound up in a dictator's hell-hole. (Harold E. Stassen)

No Natural Breaks
Farmer in swish London hotel: 'What are meal times?'
Clerk: 'Breakfast from 7 to 11, lunch from 12 to 3, tea from 4.30 to 6 and dinner from 7 till 9.'
Farmer: 'When am I going to see the town?'

Beware of Exploiters
The real problem of leisure is how to keep other people from using it.

How Tiresome
It has been left to our generation to discover that you can move heaven and earth to save five minutes and then not have the faintest idea what to do with them when you have saved them. (Dr C. E. M. Joad)

AUTOMATION

Checkmate
As the Whitehall mandarin said, 'Computers will never take over here. If they get too powerful we'll just organize them into committees.'

WE CAN TRUST THE CHAIRMAN... OLD ETONIAN!
COMPUTER STANDING COMMITTEE

Cold Comfort
The value of unemployment is that it reduces the number of jobs being replaced by automation.

Same Again
An efficiency and automation expert was called into Whitehall and started by asking questions of the staff.
'What do you do?' 'Nothing.'
'What do you do?' 'Nothing.'
'What do you do?' 'Nothing.'
'As I thought,' said the expert. 'There's too much duplication around here.'

Definition
Futurologist – A man who is worrying about what is going to replace automation.

Programmed Delay
The most up-to date excuse for failing to meet the customer's request: 'We're waiting for a reply from the computer.'

When the Computer Had its Chips
The President of IBM insisted on having their latest computer reprogrammed – after it requested to marry his daughter.

Outsmarted
Computers will never fully replace humans – they will never learn after making mistakes, how to tell us to conceal them.

Manpower Preferred
A Whitehall chief had just had a deputation from the typing pool. They said, 'Don't take on the computer which will replace twenty-five men – we'd rather have the men.'

BLOODY FOREIGNERS

Garden of Eden
Russian teacher: 'Who were the first man and woman?'
Pupil: 'Two Russians called Adam and Eve.'
Russian teacher: 'How do you know they were Russians?'
Pupil: 'That's easy, they had no clothes, no roof over their heads, only one apple between them and they called it Paradise.'

Tourism by Proxy
First British worker: 'Why do we have to put up with all these foreign tourists?'
Second British worker: 'Think of all the money they bring in.'
First British worker: 'Surely there must be some way they can stay at home and just send the money here.'

Role Found:
England is the workhouse of Europe.

Skimped
'Did you see much poverty in Britain?' asked an American of his colleague who had just returned from holiday. 'There must be some,' was his reply, 'because after staying in a London hotel I've brought a lot of it back with me.'

Accelerated Obsolescence
An Englishman was staying in a Hong Kong hotel with his wife and by chance she fell out of a window straight into the dustbin. A Chinese observing this turned to his friend and said, 'Typical Western extravagance. She good for ten years yet.'

*

UNIONS AND 'THE SYSTEM'

POLITICIANS

Maggie Stones Moss

When the TUC leaders called at Number Ten in June 1979, Moss Evans attempted to interrupt Mrs Thatcher when she was in full spate, suggesting she was less than factual. He earned a sharp reprimand. 'Mr Evans,' she said, 'not even my Cabinet Ministers talk to me like that.'

Whatever Was He Thinking Of?

Liberty and Union, now and forever, one and inseparable. (Daniel Webster, 1782–1852)

I Surrender

'The reality of industrial life is accepting that unions have greater power [and giving the unions] new responsibility to match that power.' (Edward Heath, whom the unions were responsible for throwing out of office)

Unanswerable

Heckler: 'What about the workers?'
Politician (approvingly): 'What about the workers indeed!'

Another Fix
Union chief: 'You promised me a quango job.'
Labour MP: 'There aren't any available.'
Union chief: 'You promised.'
Labour MP: 'I'll tell you what: I'll set up a committee to see why there aren't more quangos and you can be chairman.'

Revelation
Lord Curzon, the great aristocrat, when touring the trenches in the Great War, went to see the soldiers' steam baths and said as he adjusted his monocle and gazed at the mass of bodies, 'Good heavens! I had no idea that the working class had such white skins!'

Winston Churchill: A Compliment
'[The trade unions are] not mere visionaries or dreamers weaving airy utopias out of tobacco smoke.'

Dead Cert
'If you get me in your husband will have more work,' said the parliamentary candidate. 'What does your husband do?' 'He's an undertaker,' was the reply.

Only Connect
Prime Minister (on visit to factory): 'Good afternoon, my man.'
Worker: 'Forgotten my name, have you? Don't you remember me in your home village?'
Prime Minister: 'I remember your name very well but I've completely forgotten your face.'

Harold Wilson
I see no need for a Royal Commission [on trade unions] which will take minutes and waste years.

SOCIAL CONTRACTORS

Unexceptional
Incomes policy means restraint of everybody's wages except mine.

Price Cut

In 1793 Robespierre enacted the Law of the Maximum to keep food prices lower than anyone wanted to sell. Result, minimum food. As Robespierre was hauled off to the guillotine the Paris mob chanted, 'There goes the dirty maximum.'

Free Wage Bargaining When It Suits Him

Unions are performing a service to the economy by demanding wage increases of more than the five per cent stipulated by the Government. (Clive Jenkins, December 1978)

PLANNERS

Immobilized

First worker: 'Why is the factory closed, is there a strike?'

Second worker: 'No, there's a planner in the works.'

NBG

The Coal Board's Plan for coal which came out in 1956 said that there would be a shortage of coal 'for as far ahead as we can see'. Next year there was a glut.

Watch Out
Hell knows no fury like a planner scorned.

Super-cock
A planner is one who if he were a cockerel would be convinced that his crowing brought on the dawn.

Non-learners All
We're on our way, brothers. (George Brown on the National Plan which was already collapsing when he said it)

It is not planning to which we are opposed but Socialist planning. (Quintin Hogg)

Down With Smoke
At the annual conference of the Labour Party in 1978, to the dismay of those ardent regulators and controllers, Tony Benn and Ian Mikardo, who are also fervent tobacco-puffers, Labour for the first time imposed a complete ban on smoking during conference sessions.

Wet Joke
In the old days it was said that the clerks in the Foreign Office were like the fountains in Trafalgar Square because they played from ten till three.

Let Him Lump It
Did you hear of the tax inspector who showed a foreman on the lump how to fill in a tax form and the foreman repaid his kindness by showing him how to fill in a tax inspector?

Till the Pips Squeak
An American came into a London restaurant, ordered a lemon and squeezed it till it filled a glass saying, 'Beat that.' Up came an Englishman, picked up the peel, squeezed it and filled another glass. 'Who are you?' asked the American. 'I work in the Inland Revenue,' he said.

Inland Revenue Staff Solution
Some old hand has found an ingenious was to beat the Capital Transfer tax – by leaving everything to the Government.

Outsider
It is reported that when a child strayed into the Ministry of Education, no one knew what sex it was.

Clincher
An unanswerable complaint from a veteran complainer to the Dublin Board of Works ran, 'If you are my obedient servant, as you say you are, why don't you rebuild my cowshed?'

Side by Side
An official at the Ministry of Works who was looking into the design of a new lavatory seat wrote in a memo to a colleague, 'I'd like to see you on this.' 'At your convenience,' came the reply.

No Bullets to Bite
A bureaucrat in Russia wrote to his cousin in America saying that his country was no threat to peace because it didn't have any ammunition. His letter was intercepted, he was dragged before a court on a treason charge and the judge sentenced him to be hanged. 'Just as I thought,' said the bureaucrat, 'no ammunition.'

GENTS
IN CONFERENCE AND TESTING

Home from Home
Civil servant engrossed in newspapers: 'More tea please.'
Wife: 'Isn't it time you went to the office?'
Civil servant: 'I thought I was in the office.'

Numbers Game
Commons question: 'How many are working in the civil service?'
Answer: 'About one in three.'

PUBLIC CONCERNS – GENERAL

Why We Have to Lump It
A camel is a horse designed by a government committee and assembled in a nationalized workshop.

Key to Growth
A nationalized industry is one which expands by contracting debt.

What I've Always Maintained
Nationalization is the result of legislation whereby an industry becomes a regular charge on the taxpayer – as when an abandoned woman becomes a kept woman.

PUBLIC CONCERNS – BRITISH LEYLAND

Be My Guest
British Leyland have now given up the time-honoured clocking-in system and instead invite workers to sign the visitor's book.

An Example to All
Mr Bill Noggs, an assembly-line worker at British Leyland in Cowley, was today presented with a gold watch in recognition of the fact that he has worked for the company continuously without a break or time off for illness for no less than forty-five minutes.

This Takes the Biscuit
At Longbridge there is a strike in sympathy with the 400 car body workers laid off in Birmingham. Management said, 'It's not our fault, there is nothing for them to do. We only make shortbread.'

Two Finger Exercise

At Cowley this week a B.L. worker lost two fingers in an accident. Curiously enough he was unaware of the loss until he left work and waved goodbye to the foreman.

United We Boo

When Sir Keith Joseph told British Leyland workers at Cowley that the works was inefficient and deserved to be closed down immediately, 85 per cent of the audience applauded. A union spokesman said that this was because 15 per cent booed him and the other 85 per cent were applauding the 15 per cent.

Current Failure

B.L.'s electric car has met a setback – it would not travel more than four yards as the flex was not long enough.

PUBLIC CONCERNS – BRITISH RAIL

In Good Time

It is also hoped that the new machine will prove useful in clearing snow from the track. It is expected to be ready for use in this country in the summer. (Manchester paper)

Unscheduled Stop
An inter-city express suddenly halted miles from nowhere.
Passenger (to guard): 'Can I get out and pick some flowers?'
Guard: 'I can't see any flowers.'
Passenger: 'No, but I've got a packet of seeds.'

More for Your Money
Enquirer: 'Why have platform tickets gone up so?'
Information clerk: 'Because you now have a longer wait between trains.'

Non-rolling Stock
In 1974 British Rail owned 22,500 acres of 'derelict land'.

Precisely
Passenger: 'When does the ten-forty-five train leave?'
Porter: 'At exactly fifteen minutes to eleven.'

How Imaginative

An indignant protest has been lodged with a London library by British Rail, which resents the fact that in its new catalogue their timetable is classified under 'Fiction'.

A Question of Timing

Ticket collector: 'Surely this boy is over fourteen?'
Parent: 'He wasn't when he got on.'

Lesson of History

A nationalized industry invariably begins with a private loss and ends as a public liability.

No one to Ask

Interviewer: 'I'm doing a survey of passengers to find out their attitude to our service. Did you enjoy your journey?'
Passenger: 'No! I felt a bit queasy sitting with my back to the engine.'
Interviewer: 'Why didn't you ask the person sitting opposite to change seats?'
Passenger: 'Because the seat was empty.'

Put Downer
'Porter, how long will the next train be?'
'About five carriages, sir.'

Making a Meal of It
British Rail has introduced a new service for passengers. It provides breakfast in Inverness, lunch in Berwick, dinner in Oxford and your luggage in Plymouth.

Train Check
Passenger, arriving half an hour late: 'I wonder why you bother ever to publish a timetable.'
Stationmaster: 'We read timetables to know how late the trains are.'

PUBLIC CONCERNS – GAS AND CURRENT

Labour Saving
Don't kill your wife with work: let electricity do it.
(Electricity advertising slogan)

She's Got His Number
An angry subscriber having trouble with the telephone shouted at the operator, 'Am I a nutcase or are you?' The operator replied sweetly, 'I'm sorry, sir, but we don't have that information.'

PUBLIC CONCERNS – UP IN THE AIR

Hold Tight
On a flight to Egypt a passenger asked where the toilet was: 'Port side, madam,' said the steward. 'Oh dear, I don't think I can hold on till then.'

Happy Landings
Ladies and gentlemen, you have now been entirely handed over to the automatic pilot and owing to the great advance in chip technology you can relax safely in the hands of computer control. So feel free to unfasten your seat belts, your seat belts, your seat belts, your . . .

*

SUMMING UP

DEFINITIONS

Slogan
An old English substitute for argument and fact.

Socialism
Heaven if men are perfect and hell if they are not.

Stable Government
One with plenty of horse sense.

Steady Worker
One remove from motionless worker.

Success
The one sin for which there is no forgiveness.

Boss
An ingenious device installed in a factory for spotting late arrivals.

Businessman
A man who spends time making money and then spends money killing time.

Cash
The working man's credit card.

Coffee Break
Any time you can get a cup of coffee for 5p.

Coffee (or Marijuana) Break
That part of the morning when the business goes to pot.

Bank
A commercial institution which advertises its desire to serve the ordinary worker and then takes care to be open only during working hours.

Blackleg
An eccentric who attempts to treat the right to work as if it was for real.

Readjustment – When your colleague loses his job.
Recession – When you lose your job.
Depression – When your wife loses her job.

Rich Man
A poor man with money.

Rolls
Big car made by British workmen with Arab sitting inside.

Seaside
Venue for trade union annual conferences.

Self-made Man
Religious character forever praising his maker.

Sheikh
New word for everybody's employer.

LABOUR SAYS...
WISH YOU WERE HERE!

Committee
A group of men who individually can do nothing, but collectively can meet and decide that nothing can be done.

Committee Member
A privileged member of the community who has the inevitable honour of helping to maintain the fine body of men and women who man our railways.

Committee of Five
Consists of a man who does the work, three others who pat him on the back and one who brings in a minority report.

Communism
Some naïve fellows think that the essence of Communism is sharing with your neighbours, but it's not. The essence of Communism is getting your neighbours to share with you.

Compromise
The art of dividing the cake in such a way that everyone thinks he is getting the biggest piece.

Conference
– A meeting of the bored.
– Where people pass a lot of resolutions but no bars.
– What hoteliers put their revolving doors back after.

Conference Speech
A two-minute idea with a half-hour vocabulary.

Conscience Clause
An example of the kind of tolerance animating Labour's last law on governing trade unions under which only religious freaks were exempted from union membership.

Conservative
One who wants to keep your hand out of his pocket.

Democracy
A country where everybody has an equal right to feel superior to everybody else.

Director
A man who talks of birdies in the boardroom and cash flow on the course.

Discretion
What comes to those who are too old for it to do them any good.

Discussion
A pooling of ignorance.

Dividend
A certain percentage per annum perhaps.

Divisive Comment
The world is full of willing people; some willing to work, the rest willing to let them. (Robert Frost)

Economist
One who on meeting a tramp who says, 'Give us a copper, guv, I haven't eaten for three months,' replies, 'And how does that compare with the same period last year?'

A man who knows tomorrow why the things he predicted yesterday didn't happen today.

Embarrassment
Watching your boss do what you just told him couldn't be done.

Freedom Association:
A worthy body which supports freedom of non-association.

Freedom of Association
The freedom to join a union even if you don't want to, provided the union will have you; the freedom of union officials to refuse or withdraw a union card when it is a condition of employment.

Good Executive
One who never puts off till tomorrow what he can get someone else to do today.

Good Idea
One that the boss is convinced he thought of first.

Good Negotiator
A man who can convince his wife that all she really needs is an umbrella when she thinks she wants a fur coat.

Good Race Relations
Not calling a spade a spade.

Good Teacher
One who could be a super teacher if she had a little class.

Greedy Capitalist
Trade union leader manqué.

Genius
Any General Secretary of the Transport and General Workers Union.

Hospital
Establishment which carries out periodic endurance tests on its inmates (supervised by the National Union of Public Employees) in order to bring home to people the truth of the Darwinian maxim that it is only the fittest who survive.

IBM
The place that launched a million chips.

Income Tax Forms
Blankety Blanks.

Inland Revenue
The country's most successful mail-order business.

High Government Official
Bureaucrat who has drunk too much.

Industrial Tribunal
A kind of welfare bank from which workers collect a bonus for being sacked.

Integrity
In an executive means readiness to share the credit with the chap who did the work.

Keen Worker
One who looks for something to do after he's got a job.

Lame Duck
Business in the salvaging of which a politician often cooks his goose.

Living Wage
Any income that is at least £5 a week more than that of your wife's sister's husband.

An elastic concept depending on whether the speaker is giving or receiving it.

Matrimony
The only union which permits a woman to work unlimited overtime without extra pay.

Moderate
A man who makes enemies left and right.

Occupational Disease
When work makes you sick.